# VOLCANOES

Paul Mason

A+

Smart Apple Media
P.O. Box 3263
Mankato, MN, 56002

First published in 2011 by
MACMILLAN EDUCATION AUSTRALIA PTY LTD
15–19 Claremont St, South Yarra, Australia 3141

Visit our web site at www.macmillan.com.au or go directly to www.macmillanlibrary.com.au

Associated companies and representatives throughout the world.

Library of Congress Cataloging-in-Publication Data has been applied for.

Publisher: Carmel Heron
Commissioning Editor: Niki Horin
Managing Editor: Vanessa Lanaway
Editors: Philip Bryan and Tim Clarke
Proofreader: Kylie Cockle
Designer: Cristina Neri, Canary Graphic Design
Page layout: Cristina Neri, Canary Graphic Design
Photo researcher: Jes Senbergs (management: Debbie Gallagher)
Illustrator: Peter Bull Art Studio
Production Controller: Vanessa Johnson

Manufactured in China by Macmillan Production (Asia) Ltd.
Kwun Tong, Kowloon, Hong Kong
Supplier Code: CP January 2011

**Acknowledgments**
The publisher would like to thank volcanologist Dr Adele Bear-Crozier from Geoscience Australia for her assistance in reviewing these manuscripts.

The author and publisher are grateful to the following for permission to reproduce copyright material:

Front cover photograph: Lights of Catania are outstretched beneath an erupting Piano del Lago, courtesy of Getty Images/Carsten Peter.

Photographs courtesy of: AAP Image/AP Photo Karen Prinsloo, **14**; Dreamstime/Julien Gron, **24**, /Ollrig, **18**; Getty Images/AFP, **20**, **27**, **28**, **29**, /Philippe Bourseiller/Image Bank, **7**, /Nordic Photos, **5**; iStockPhoto/ Warren Goldswain, **4**, / Valerie Koch, **26**, /Floriano Rescigno, **13**,/Rusm, **22**, /Dave Wetzel, **21**; MSF/Miguel Cuenca, **12**; National Library of Australia, **11**; Photolibrary/The Bridgeman Art Library, Chichester Canal, c.1829, Turner, Joseph Mallord William (1775-1851) / Petworth House, Sussex, UK, **15**; Photolibrary/Science Photo Library/JeremyBishop, **16**, /Royal Astronomical Society, **17**; USGS, **19**.

**Please Note**
At the time of printing, the Internet addresses appearing in this book were correct. Owing to the dynamic nature of the Internet, however, we cannot guarantee that all these addresses will remain correct.

# CONTENTS

**DISASTER WORDS**

When a word is printed in **bold**,
look for its meaning in the
"Disaster Words" box.

# DISASTER WATCH

*Natural disasters can destroy whole areas and kill thousands of people. The only protection from them is to go on disaster watch. This means knowing the warning signs that a disaster might be about to happen, and having a plan for what to do if one strikes.*

We cannot stop natural disasters from happening, but being prepared can help minimize the harm caused by a disaster.

## What Are Natural Disasters?

Natural disasters are nature's most damaging events. They include wildfires, earthquakes, extreme storms, floods, tsunamis (say *soon-ah-meez*), and volcanic eruptions.

## Preparing for Natural Disasters

Preparing for natural disasters helps us to reduce their effects in three key ways, by:

- increasing our chances of survival
- making our homes as disaster-proof as possible
- reducing the long-term effects of the disaster.

# VOLCANOES

Volcanoes occur in places where extremely hot rock breaks through the surface of Earth. When this happens it is called a volcanic eruption. These are among nature's most extreme events. People die as a result of volcanic eruptions every year. More than 500 million people live near volcanoes. These people need to be prepared for an eruption, and to know what to do if one happens.

## About Volcanic Eruptions

A volcanic eruption happens when the Earth's surface opens. The opening releases dangerous materials, including **lava**, poisonous gas, and huge clouds of ash.

## Preparing for an Eruption

There are three key ways to prepare for an eruption. You must know:

- the warning signs that a volcano might be about to erupt, and how to react
- how to get to safety as fast as possible
- the challenges facing those who survive a volcanic eruption.

## The 2010 Eyjafjallajökull eruption

**Date**: April 14, 2010

**Location**: Eyjafjallajökull Glacier, Iceland

The surprise 2010 eruption of Iceland's Eyjafjallajökull volcano brought flooding to Iceland, as hot lava melted a glacier. The volcano's ash cloud stopped aircraft across Europe from flying, stranding many people.

The Eyjafjallajökull volcano in Iceland erupted in 2010.

# WHERE DO VOLCANIC ERUPTIONS HAPPEN?

*Volcanoes that are likely to erupt are known as "active" volcanoes. Most of these dangerous volcanoes are found around the edges of the Pacific Ocean, but there are active volcanoes all around the world – some of them very close to large cities.*

## The Ring of fire

The circle of coastlines around the Pacific Ocean is often called the "Ring of Fire," because more than half of the world's active volcanoes are found there. The ring stretches along the western Pacific Ocean from New Zealand, through northern New Guinea, Indonesia, and Japan. Then it arcs eastward along the Aleutian Islands, before following the west coasts of North and South America southward.

### EYEWITNESS WORDS

Iceland's Gunar Gestur Geirmundsson witnessed the sudden eruption of the Eyjafjallajökull volcano in Iceland in 2010:

*"I could see another awesome explosion about 15 minutes ago, which sent more ash into the sky toward Western Europe."*

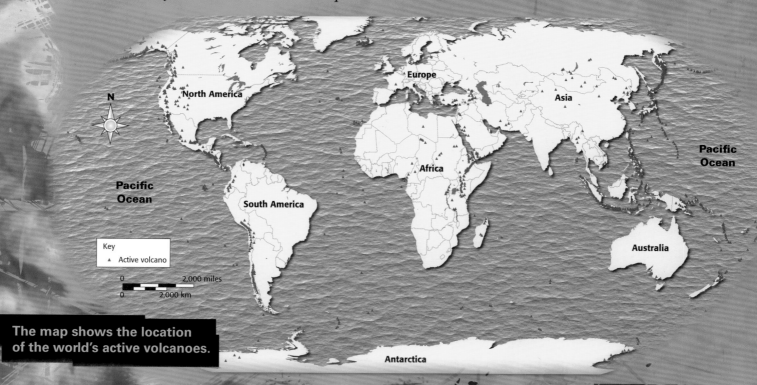

**Key**
▲ Active volcano

0        2,000 miles
0      2,000 km

The map shows the location of the world's active volcanoes.

## Other Disaster Watch Areas

There are many areas outside the Ring of Fire that contain active volcanoes. These include:

- the mid-Pacific Ocean, especially the Hawaiian Islands (which are actually the tips of giant undersea volcanoes)
- the Arabian Peninsula and the east coast of Africa, where a line of volcanoes stretches down the Red Sea coast of Saudi Arabia and along Africa's Rift Valley
- the Indian Ocean, especially in the northeast, along Indonesia's coastline
- the eastern Mediterranean Sea, especially Italy, Greece, and the Middle East
- Iceland, which was formed by volcanoes.

On the island of Hawaii, lava from the Kilauea volcano flows into the Pacific Ocean. The islands were formed by volcanic eruptions, and as new eruptions occur, the island is growing.

## The Most Disastrous Volcanic Eruptions

Volcanic eruptions cause the greatest disasters when they happen in areas where many people live. Volcanic soil is good for growing crops, so the land near volcanoes is often prized. The people who live nearby have to balance the benefits of the rich soil against the risk of a volcanic eruption.

### The Eight Deadliest Volcanic Eruptions

| Rank | Year | Location | Estimated Total Deaths |
|------|------|----------|------------------------|
| 1 | 1816 | Mt Tambora, Indonesia | 92,000 |
| 2 | 1883 | Mt Krakatau, Indonesia | 36,000 |
| 3 | 1902 | Mt Pelée, Martinique | 30,000 |
| 4 | 1985 | Nevado del Ruiz, Colombia | 23,000 |
| 5 | 1792 | Mt Unzen, Japan | 15,000 |
| 6 | 79 AD | Mt Vesuvius, Italy | 10,000–25,000 |
| 7 | 1783–4 | Laki, Iceland | 9,350 |
| 8 | 1631 | Mt Vesuvius, Italy | 6,000 |

# WHAT CAUSES VOLCANIC ERUPTIONS?

*Volcanic eruptions are caused by weaknesses in Earth's crust. Earth's crust is made up of tectonic plates. Eruptions occur where these tectonic plates meet, or where there are holes in the plates.*

## DISASTER WORDS

**tectonic plates** giant sheets of rock that make up Earth's surface

**magma** liquid rock deep within Earth

**lava** liquid rock that flows from a volcano

## Movement of Tectonic Plates

Eruptions at the edges of tectonic plates happen because either the plates are pulling apart or pushing together.

### Pulling Apart

As tectonic plates pull apart, **magma** erupts up through the gap. This cools and hardens, forming volcanic ridges of new rock. This type of eruption often happens under the ocean floor, such as in the middle of the Atlantic Ocean.

### Pushing Together

As one tectonic plate slides beneath the other, magma is created. Sometimes the magma erupts to the surface as **lava**. Most volcanoes in the Ring of Fire have been formed by plates pushing together.

Earth's crust is made up of a series of sheets of rock, called tectonic plates. Volcanoes usually occur where these plates meet.

Key
— Tectonic plate boundary

N

North America

Europe

Asia

Africa

South America

Australia

Antarctica

0    2,000 miles
0    2,000 km

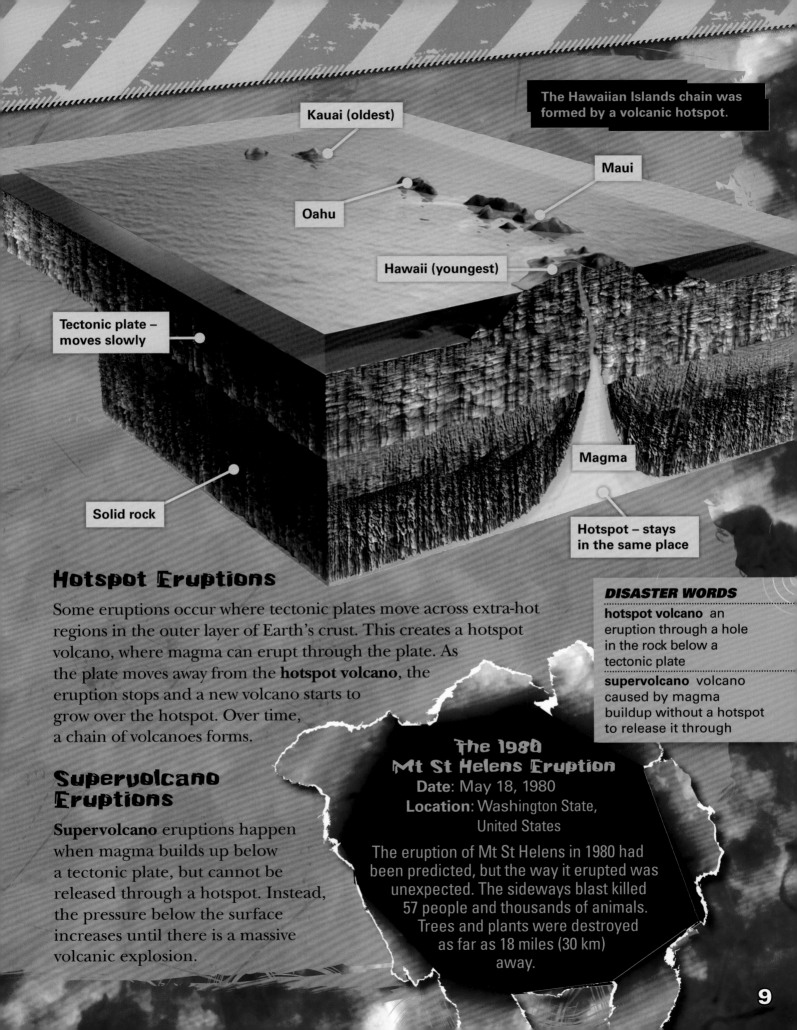

Kauai (oldest)

Maui

Oahu

Hawaii (youngest)

Tectonic plate – moves slowly

Magma

Solid rock

Hotspot – stays in the same place

## Hotspot Eruptions

Some eruptions occur where tectonic plates move across extra-hot regions in the outer layer of Earth's crust. This creates a hotspot volcano, where magma can erupt through the plate. As the plate moves away from the **hotspot volcano**, the eruption stops and a new volcano starts to grow over the hotspot. Over time, a chain of volcanoes forms.

## Supervolcano Eruptions

**Supervolcano** eruptions happen when magma builds up below a tectonic plate, but cannot be released through a hotspot. Instead, the pressure below the surface increases until there is a massive volcanic explosion.

### DISASTER WORDS

**hotspot volcano** an eruption through a hole in the rock below a tectonic plate

**supervolcano** volcano caused by magma buildup without a hotspot to release it through

### The 1980 Mt St Helens Eruption

**Date**: May 18, 1980
**Location**: Washington State, United States

The eruption of Mt St Helens in 1980 had been predicted, but the way it erupted was unexpected. The sideways blast killed 57 people and thousands of animals. Trees and plants were destroyed as far as 18 miles (30 km) away.

# DO ALL VOLCANOES ERUPT IN THE SAME WAY?

*Most volcanic eruptions begin with similar kinds of activity. However, volcanoes come in a variety of shapes and sizes, and each type of volcano usually erupts in a different way.*

**DISASTER WORDS**

**volcanologists** scientists who study volcanoes

**tremors** shaking movements

**harmonic tremors** vibrations of rock caused by the movement of magma

## Warning Signs

Most volcanoes give off warning signs that an eruption is beginning. **Volcanologists** know an eruption could be brewing inside the volcano when they start to notice:

- earth **tremors**, which are minor earthquakes that most people do not even notice
- changes to the volcano's surface, such as bulges of rock that suddenly begin to grow
- increases in the amount of gas or steam being released from the volcano
- an increase in **harmonic tremors**.

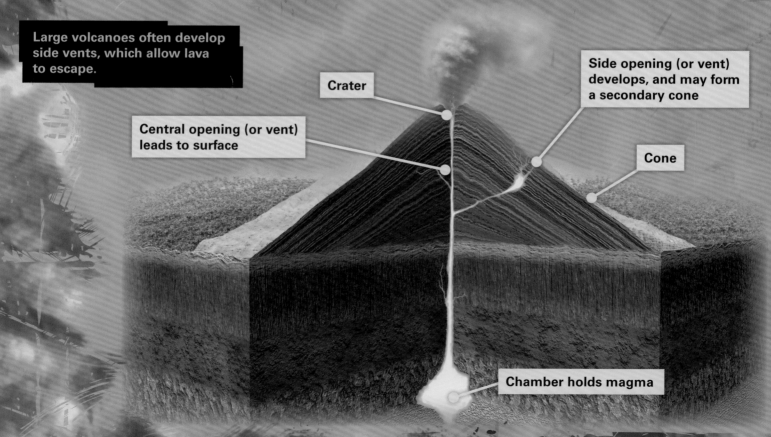

Large volcanoes often develop side vents, which allow lava to escape.

Crater

Side opening (or vent) develops, and may form a secondary cone

Central opening (or vent) leads to surface

Cone

Chamber holds magma

The eruption of Mt Lamington in Papua New Guinea in 1951 caused deaths and devastation as far as 8 miles (14 km) away.

# Different Types of Eruption

The force of an eruption and its effects depend on the type of volcano. There are four main types of volcano and they each erupt in different ways:

- Shield volcanoes have a low, flat shape. The lava from a shield volcano's eruption may flow a long way, but these volcanoes rarely explode violently.
- Lava dome volcanoes can produce violent explosions, but the lava rarely flows far.
- **Stratovolcanoes** are the shape most people think of as a volcano. They often erupt violently and have been responsible for many of history's most disastrous eruptions.
- Supervolcanoes are explosions of giant magma chambers that are thousands of times bigger than any other volcanoes. Fortunately, the last supervolcanic explosion was 640,000 years ago!

## The 1951 Mt Lamington Eruption

**Date**: January 18 and 21, 1951
**Location**: Oro Province, Papua New Guinea

The violent eruption of Mt Lamington, Papua New Guinea, on January 21, 1951 took local people by surprise. Many people had not even realized the mountain was a volcano until the minor eruption three days earlier. The volcano continued to erupt for the next six weeks, making it difficult to rescue the survivors. The eruption is estimated to have killed more than 3,000 people.

**DISASTER WORDS**

**stratovolcanoes** tall, cone-shaped volcanoes

# WHAT IS A VOLCANIC ERUPTION LIKE?

*Volcanoes erupt when pressure builds up deep below Earth's surface. The pressure becomes strong enough to burst through the **tectonic plates**, releasing a variety of volcanic materials onto the surface.*

## Volcanic Products

If a nearby volcano erupts, there are several key **volcanic products** people could be faced with, including lava, rocks, ash, mud, and gas.

### Lava

Lava is molten rock. It is released at temperatures between 1,300 °F and 2,200 °F (700 °C and 1,200 °C) and can flow a long way from the eruption, sometimes very quickly. However, lava usually flows slowly enough for people to escape from it – as long as their escape route is not cut off.

The Nyiragongo volcano (pictured) in Zaire (now Democratic Republic of Congo) erupted in 1977. Lava flowed downhill at up to 60 miles (100 km) per hour.

## Clouds of Tephra

Any solid material thrown into the air during a volcanic eruption is referred to as tephra. Tephra includes ash, pea-sized rocks, and large stones. Ash clouds from volcanoes can spread through the atmosphere and affect weather patterns around the world.

## Lahar

Lahar is a mixture of mud, water, tephra, and gas. Lahars can flow downhill at up to 60 miles (100 km) per hour, and have been known to cover entire towns.

## Pyroclastic Flows

Pyroclastic flows combine tephra and hot gases. They can spread at speeds of up to 430 miles (700 km) per hour, and reach temperatures of 1,800 °F (1,000 °C). In 1902, pyroclastic flows from the eruption of Mt Pelée in Martinique killed 30,000 people.

## Poisonous Gases

Poisonous gases cause a small percentage of volcano-related deaths (roughly three deaths in every 100).

This plaster cast is of a man who died in the 79 AD eruption of Mt Vesuvius in Italy. He covered his mouth to try and avoid choking on the ash and poisonous gases ejected during the eruption.

## The Volcanic Explosivity Index

| VEI | Volume of Tephra, km³ | Famous Examples |
| --- | --- | --- |
| 0 | Less than 0.00001 | |
| 1 | Up to 0.001 | Nyiragongo, Zaire/DRC, 2002 |
| 2 | Up to 0.01 | Whakaari/White Island, New Zealand, 2001 |
| 3 | Up to 0.1 | Mt Etna, Italy, 2002–03 |
| 4 | Up to 1 | Chaitén, Chile, 2008 |
| 5 | Up to 10 | Mt St Helens, United States, 1980 |
| 6 | Up to 100 | Mt Pinatubo, The Philippines, 1991 |
| 7 | More than 100 | Mt Tambora, Indonesia, 1815 |
| 8 | More than 1,000 | Yellowstone supervolcano, 60,000 years ago |

The Volcanic Explosivity Index (VEI) was invented in 1982. It measures the strength of a volcanic eruption by the amount of material the eruption produces.

# WHAT DAMAGE DO VOLCANOES CAUSE?

*The 1883 volcanic eruption of Krakatau, Indonesia, was roughly 13,000 times as powerful as the first atomic bomb. Even much smaller volcanic eruptions cause extensive damage to people, animals, and the natural environment.*

## DISASTER WORDS

**volcanic products** items created or released by a volcanic eruption

**lava** liquid rock that flows from a volcano

**lahars** volcanic mudflow

**decompose** rot away

**pyroclastic flows** hot, dense flows of volcanic ash, gas and debris collected from the ground's surface

## Human Impact

Volcanic eruptions kill people every year. However, volcanoes also affect people in other ways, by spreading disease, damaging property, and ruining crops.

## Death and Disease

**Volcanic products**, such as **lava**, **lahars**, and ash, lead to the deaths of many people. Disease is a problem for the survivors, as dead bodies rapidly **decompose**, especially during hot weather. They can poison water supplies and spread disease in other ways.

## Damage to Property

Huge areas can be destroyed by a big volcanic eruption. Lava flows and lahars bury buildings, and **pyroclastic flows** flatten and burn everything near the eruption, destroying people's homes and businesses.

## Ruined Crops

Everything growing within the volcano's reach will be buried or burned, including crops and livestock. This can result in food shortages for people living nearby.

In January, 2002, the eruption of the Nyiragongo volcano devastated the Goma area of Eastern Congo. These men are searching through wreckage in the central business district.

# Environmental Impact

The environmental impact of volcanic eruptions can be divided into immediate effects on animals and plants and mid- to long-term effects on the climate.

## Effects on Animals and Plants

The immediate effects on animals and plants are the same as for humans: many die, and surviving animals are left without homes. The local **ecosystem** is buried under lava, mud or ash, burned, or flattened.

## Effects on the Climate

Major volcanic eruptions eject so much gas and ash into the atmosphere that it affects the weather and climate. Sunlight is blocked and the temperature drops. The volcanic eruptions of Laki (1783), Tambora (1815), Krakatau (1883), and Pinatubo (1991) all seem to have led to significant global cooling.

Volcanic ash in Earth's atmosphere can cause spectacular sunsets in the surrounding countries, such as this one in this nineteenth-century painting of Chichester canal in England.

## The 1815 Mt Tambora Eruption

**Date**: April, 1815
**Location**: Lesser Sunda Islands, Indonesia

The 1815 eruption of Mt Tambora in Indonesia was heard more than 125 miles (200 km) away. Sulfur gas poured into the atmosphere and Earth's climate temporarily cooled. The year 1816 was the second-coldest northern year recorded, and became known as "The Year Without Summer."

**DISASTER WORDS**

**ecosystem** area where the plants, animals, and climate are all interconnected

# DETECTING VOLCANIC ERUPTIONS

*Volcanic eruptions cannot be predicted before they begin. However, **volcanologists** can sometimes detect the beginning of an eruption long before the explosion at the surface happens. They do this by looking at how the volcano is behaving, and its history.*

## DISASTER WORDS

**volcanologists** scientists who study volcanoes

**seismic** earth-shaking

**tremors** shaking movements

**harmonic tremors** vibrations caused by the movement of magma

**magma** liquid rock deep within Earth

**evacuated** left a dangerous area

**samples** small amounts of something that will be taken away for testing

## Measuring Volcanic Activity

Increases in volcanic activity can signal that a volcano is getting ready to erupt. When trying to predict an eruption, volcanologists look at:

- the amount of **seismic** activity, such as **tremors**, and **harmonic tremors**. These might show that **magma** is moving.
- whether the volcano is changing shape. For example, new bulges of rock on the sides can show that pressure is building up inside
- the amount of steam and gas (particularly sulfur dioxide) that the volcano produces. If this increases, it may show that an eruption has begun.

### EYEWITNESS WORDS

Gina Christie lived near the Eyjafjallajökull volcano, Iceland, when it erupted in 2010:

*"We are still on alert but have not been **evacuated**. We are luckier than those in surrounding areas as our village is not under direct threat at the moment."*

A volcanologist at work, taking **samples** from Mount Etna in Italy.

## Volcano Diary

A "volcano diary" is a scientific record of how a volcano behaves each day. Each of the world's most dangerous volcanoes has a volcano diary. Over time, the diary reveals whether there is a pattern to their eruptions.

This engraving shows Mt Etna erupting in 1637. Knowledge of how Mt Etna behaved in the past helps today's volcanologists work out if a new eruption is coming.

# Historical Information

A volcano's history is used to assess whether it may be about to erupt. If a volcano starts to behave just as it did the last time it erupted, another eruption could be coming. Information about a volcano's history comes from taking samples and consulting historical records.

## Taking Samples

Volcanologists take samples of surrounding rocks and other material from the volcano. They want to find out where explosions happened in the past, where **side vents** could open, and the direction taken by **lava** flows.

## Historical Records

Volcanologists consult historical records to build up a picture of how the volcano acted during previous eruptions.

# MONITORING VOLCANOES

There are about 1,500 active volcanoes in the world, and the world's 16 most dangerous volcanoes are constantly monitored for signs of an eruption. Other volcanoes are monitored only after they have started to erupt.

## DISASTER WORDS

**volcanologists** scientists who study volcanoes

**seismographs** instruments that measure ground vibrations

**magma** liquid rock deep within Earth

**spectrometers** instruments that measure how much of a particular gas is in the air

## Before a Volcanic Eruption

Before an eruption, **volcanologists** use a variety of tools to determine how a volcano is behaving. Among the tools are:

- **seismographs**, which measure movements below Earth's surface and warn that **magma** may be on the move
- GPS (global positioning system) and other devices that can record changes in Earth's surface, warning that pressure is building up
- **spectrometers** to measure the amounts of gas that the volcano releases, such as carbon dioxide and sulfur dioxide.

### EYEWITNESS WORDS

Father Buencuchillo, a priest, witnessed the eruption of Mt Taal, Philippines, in 1754:

*"The columns of fire and smoke ascended (rose) higher than ever before… the whole island [was] covered by the smoke and the glowing rocks and ashes. All this was accompanied by terrific lightning and thunder above, and violent shocks of earthquakes underneath."*

Where towns and cities are near volcanoes, the volcano's activity must be carefully monitored. The town of Centuripe in Sicily is close to Mount Etna.

# When an Eruption Begins

Once an eruption has started, volcanologists retreat to a safe distance. They try to record as much information as possible in the hope that it will be useful in the future. Volcanologists leave devices on the volcano, which may not survive the eruption, and monitor **seismic** activity from farther away. Combined with timed video evidence, this creates a useful record of events.

## Decade Volcanoes

"Decade volcanoes" are volcanoes that international volcanologists have decided need to be watched most closely. These volcanoes have either had extremely powerful eruptions in the past, or may have them in the future. People often choose to live in volcanic areas because the soil there tends to be especially good for growing crops, so the Decade volcanoes are also close to populated areas. If any of the Decade volcanoes erupted without warning, the consequences could be disastrous.

This map shows the locations of the 16 Decade volcanoes.

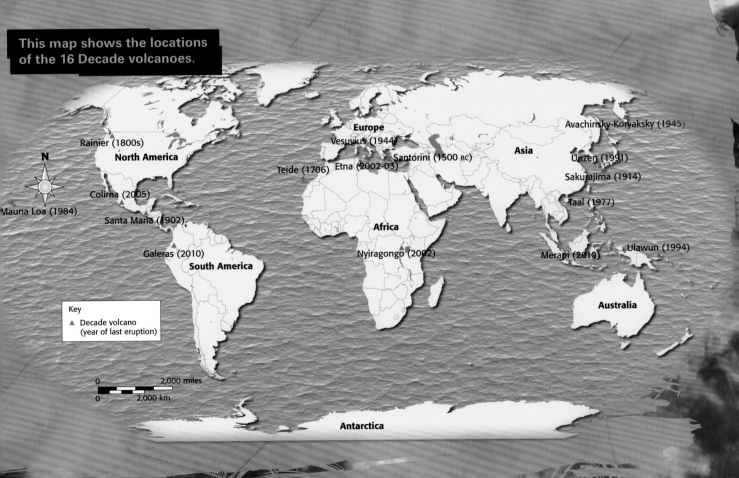

N

Rainier (1800s)
**North America**
Colima (2005)
Mauna Loa (1984)
Santa Maria (1902)
Galeras (2010)
**South America**

**Europe**
Vesuvius (1944)
Teide (1706) Etna (2002-03)
Santorini (1500 BC)
**Africa**
Nyiragongo (2002)

Avachinsky-Koryaksky (1945)
**Asia**
Unzen (1991)
Sakurajima (1914)
Taal (1977)
Merapi (2010)
Ulawun (1994)

**Australia**

Key
▲ Decade volcano
(year of last eruption)

0          2,000 miles
0     2,000 km

**Antarctica**

# WHEN A VOLCANO ERUPTS

**When a volcano erupts, the first thing the government and emergency services do is warn people to get to a safe location. Next, they may attempt to limit the damage the eruption causes. Then they start preparing a *relief effort*.**

## DISASTER WORDS

**relief effort** help for people in difficulty

**volcanologists** scientists who study volcanoes

**lava** liquid rock that flows from a volcano

**lahars** volcanic mudflows

**evacuate** leave a dangerous area

## Eruption Warnings

Based on advice from **volcanologists**, the authorities issue warnings to people who could be affected by the eruption.

## Local Warnings

The authorities use radio and TV to let people in specific areas know if they are at a particularly high level of risk. For example, some homes may be on a likely route for **lava** or **lahars**. The authorities issue warnings that people should **evacuate** if they are in immediate danger.

## National and International Warnings

Volcanic eruptions affect the safety of people far from the volcano. Clouds of volcanic ash can be blown thousands of miles by the wind. In 2010, a cloud of ash from an eruption in Iceland stopped aircraft from flying across Northern Europe and the Atlantic Ocean.

These children at Legok, Indonesia, are practicing their school's volcano emergency drill so that they know what to do when a volcano erupts.

## Limiting Damage

With an eruption underway, attempts may be made to limit the damage it causes. For example, giant barriers can be used to divert lava flows away from towns. When this failed at Mt Etna, Italy, in 1991, helicopters dropped huge blocks of concrete into the volcano, halting the flow of lava before it reached the town of Zafferana.

## Preparing a Relief Effort

The authorities begin to prepare a possible relief effort. They put the **emergency services** and defense forces on alert. Once it is safe to do so, they will deal with any casualties, bring in essential supplies and help get life back to normal as soon as possible.

Some volcanoes have warning signs nearby, letting people know the level of threat posed by the volcano.

**DANGER**

VOLCANIC FUMES ARE HAZARDOUS TO YOUR HEALTH AND MAY BE LIFE THREATENING

DO NOT ENTER THIS AREA IF YOU ARE A PERSON AT RISK

- RESPIRATORY PROBLEMS
- HEART PROBLEMS
- PREGNANT
- INFANTS & YOUNG CHILDREN

### The 2006 Mt Merapi Eruptions

**Date**: April–June, 2006
**Location**: Central Java, Indonesia

Mt Merapi in Indonesia is one of the world's most closely monitored volcanoes. In May 2006, earthquakes prompted the local people to evacuate, but there was no volcanic eruption. In October and November, 2010, Merapi *did* erupt. Despite warning sirens sounding to alert the local people, there were more than 100 deaths.

# ARE YOU AT RISK?

Are you and your family at risk from a volcanic eruption? Your local library and council offices, and the Internet, are good places to start to investigate the area where you are living or staying.

## Key Questions

Measure the risk from a volcanic eruption by asking key questions about an area's volcanic history, and whether there are preparations in place in case a volcano erupts. Ask the following questions about where you live, or where you are vacationing.

### Are there Volcanoes in the Area? Are They Active?

If there are active volcanoes within 6 miles (10 km), the risks from an eruption will increase. If there is no volcano within 60 miles (100 km), the risks are low.

### Has There Ever Been an Eruption Here before?

If there has been a previous eruption, however long ago, there could be another one. For example, Vesuvius in Italy is on the Decade volcano list even though its last giant eruption was almost 2,000 years ago.

Roughly five million tourists visit Tenerife in the Canary Islands each year, taking their vacation in the shadow of Mt Teide, a Decade volcano.

### The Soufrière Hills Eruptions

Date: 1995, 1997, 2006, 2008
Location: Montserrat, Caribbean Sea

The Soufrière Hills volcano on the Island of Montserrat is one of the world's most active volcanoes. Since 1995, eruptions have destroyed the capital city, buried the island's airport, and caused the **evacuation** of more than 65 percent of residents. The once-booming tourist industry has been wrecked.

## Did Previous Eruptions Affect the Area You Are Visiting?

If lava flows or other **volcanic products** did not previously affect your area, it is at less risk. Even so, be vigilant: volcanoes do not always behave in exactly the same way. A place that escaped damage last time may not escape it next time.

## What Kind of Eruption Was it? Did it Happen Quickly or Slowly?

Some volcanoes, such as Mauna Loa, Hawaii, tend to erupt with slow lava flows rather than explosions. This gives people time to evacuate to safety. (Even so, Mauna Loa has sometimes erupted explosively, so the risk is lessened, not eliminated.)

## What Plans and Precautions Are Already in Place in Case of an Eruption?

If there are warning systems in place, and you have your own personal plan for what to do if the volcano erupts, your risks will be reduced further.

N

0 — 10 miles
0 — 10 km

Auburn

Tacoma

Puyallup

White River

Greenwater

Wilkeson

Carbonado

Carbon River

Puyallup River

Eatonville

Nisqually River

Mount Rainier

Elbe    Ashford

**Legend:**
- Small lahars, likely to happen less than every 100 years
- Medium-sized lahars, likely to happen every 100–500 years
- Large lahars, likely to happen every 500–1,000 years
- Areas likely to be affected by lava or pyroclastic flows

This is a volcanic hazard map for Mt Rainier in Washington State, United States. It shows the areas most likely to be affected by **lahars**, **lava**, and **pyroclastic flows**.

# TOP TIPS FOR REDUCING RISK

*If you live or stay in an area where there are volcanic eruptions, the risks can never be completely removed, however hard the authorities work. However, making your own preparations will decrease the risks still further.*

## DISASTER WORDS

**evacuate** leave a dangerous area

**lava** liquid rock that flows from a volcano

**pyroclastic flows** hot, dense flows of volcanic ash, gas and debris collected from the ground's surface

## Volcano Myths

Believing some of these myths about volcanoes could cost you your life.

1 *The most dangerous thing about a volcano is the lava.*

False. Far more people are killed by ash and **pyroclastic flows**.

2 *Lava only flows slowly.*

False. Most lava flows slowly, but some lava flows extremely fast – certainly faster than you can run.

3 *If a volcano has not erupted for a long time, it never will erupt again.*

False. It may not be likely to erupt, but that is not the same as saying it will not erupt.

4 *If lots of people live near a volcano, it must be safe.*

False. The opposite is just as likely to be true.

5 *Volcanoes with guided tours must be safe to visit.*

False. Many volcanologists and adventurers have been killed exploring volcanoes.

## Preparing an Emergency Plan

The only way to stay safe from a volcanic eruption is to **evacuate** the area that might be affected. The government or emergency services will tell people to evacuate if the danger level is high. An effective evacuation relies on careful planning and good timing.

To work well, an evacuation plan needs to be clear, and rehearsed by everyone who will be using it. Include these key items:

- Where will everyone meet up?
- Which evacuation route will you take? Hazard maps and advice from the local council may help your planning.

Make sure there are back-up options for each stage, in case the original meeting point or evacuation route is impossible to reach.

**Lava** races down the mountainside during an eruption.

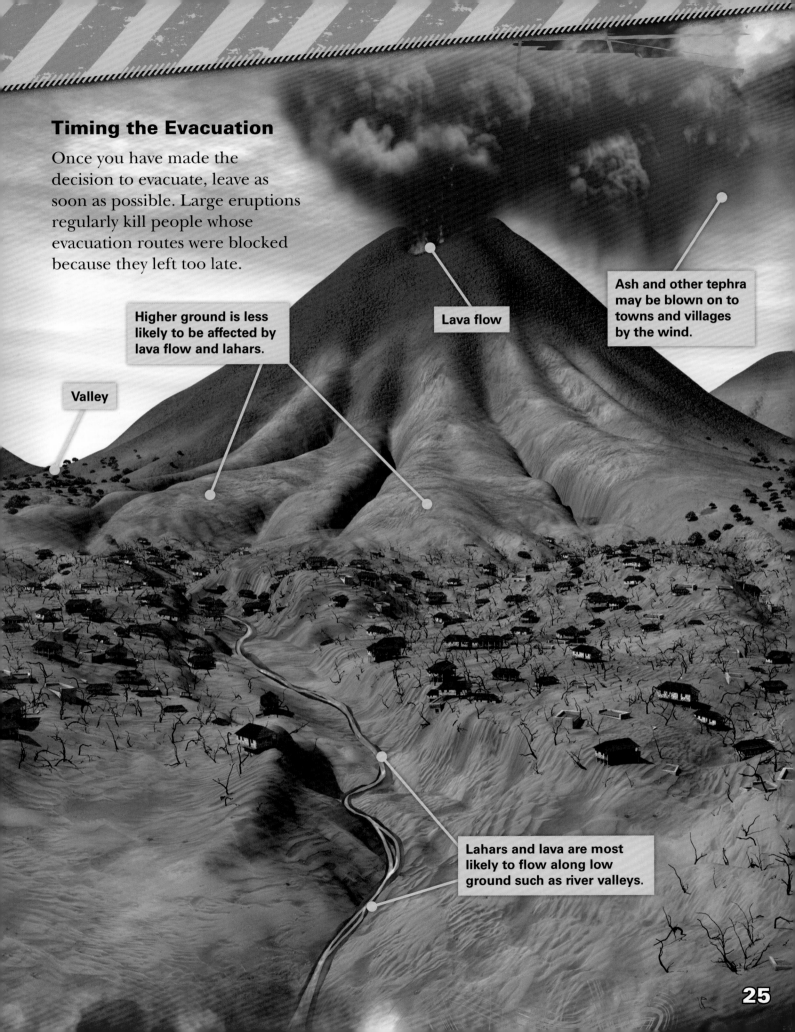

## Timing the Evacuation

Once you have made the decision to evacuate, leave as soon as possible. Large eruptions regularly kill people whose evacuation routes were blocked because they left too late.

**Higher ground is less likely to be affected by lava flow and lahars.**

**Lava flow**

**Ash and other tephra may be blown on to towns and villages by the wind.**

**Valley**

**Lahars and lava are most likely to flow along low ground such as river valleys.**

# WHAT YOU CAN DO IF A VOLCANO ERUPTS

*If a volcano erupts unexpectedly, or before you have had time to **evacuate**, following a few simple guidelines could save your life. Stay calm and try to think through your options as clearly as possible. Be ready to adapt your plans if necessary.*

## DISASTER WORDS

**evacuate** leave a dangerous area

**lava** liquid rock that flows from a volcano

**pyroclastic flows** hot, dense flows of volcanic ash, gas and debris collected from the ground's surface

**lahar** volcanic mudflow

## When an Eruption Has Started

Once an eruption begins, and assuming it is too late to evacuate to safety:

1. Make your way to a secure, solid building with a strong 'A-frame' roof, as you will need to shelter indoors.
2. Avoid low-lying ground, which is likely to be affected by **lava** and **pyroclastic flows**.
3. If possible, avoid bridges that could be swept away in a fast-moving **lahar**.

Once a volcano erupts, lava can quickly block roads and bridges, making evacuation difficult and dangerous.

### Volcano Emergency Kit

A volcano emergency kit contains essential items, is light enough to carry, and is easy to grab in an emergency. It should contain food and water for a week and a first-aid kit. You could also add:
- wind-up torch and radio
- multi-tool, including a can-opener
- cash to last at least a week
- cell phone and charged spare battery.

Ash from the 2008 Chaiten volcanic eruption half-buried houses in Santiago, Chile. Residents evacuated, but if they had not been able to leave and remained indoors, they may have remained safe.

## Once you Are Indoors

Once you are indoors, remain indoors.
1. Save water in baths, basins, and buckets, as the water supply might be limited in the next few days.
2. If the volcano is releasing volcanic ash, stay inside and keep your doors and windows closed. Seal doors and windows against the ash using wet towels or blankets.
3. Do not lie on the floor or ground because carbon dioxide, one of the most poisonous volcanic gases, collects there.

### EYEWITNESS WORDS

Geologist Jeff Marso was almost caught by a lahar in Guatemala, in 1989:

*"The lahar passed below us at what seemed an incredible speed … We decided that we were not high enough and ran for the safety of the far bank. There, ground vibrations made it difficult to stand and we had to shout to be heard over the roar."*

# AFTER AN ERUPTION

*The danger from a volcano does not end when it stops erupting. The volcano could still be dangerous, and further eruptions might happen. Always wait to hear the official all-clear before going outside. Even when this is finally given, there will be other dangers to consider.*

## Once the All-Clear is Given

When the authorities say it is safe to go out, follow a few simple guidelines to keep your family safe.

## Cover your nose, mouth, and eyes

A breathing mask is ideal, and goggles will keep the ash out of your eyes and lungs. If inhaled, the ash can cause breathing difficulties, especially for babies and old people.

### EYEWITNESS WORDS

In 2010, Icelander Gina Christie knew that the eruption of Eyjafjallajökull could trigger another volcanic eruption:

*"If Katla [a nearby volcano] explodes, it will do so with no warning and it will make the eruption from Eyjafjallajökull look like a storm in a teacup."*

After the eruption of the Chaiten volcano in Santiago, Chile, in May, 2008, survivors wore cloth masks to stop ash getting into their lungs.

Soldiers from the Chilean army helped to clear ash from the roofs of buildings after the eruption of the Chaiten volcano.

## Remove Ash from Roofs

Clear rain gutters and roofs of volcanic ash. Volcanic ash is very heavy, and can cause buildings to collapse. It can also become like concrete if it gets wet, then dries.

## Keep Ash Outside Buildings

Volcanic ash is difficult to get rid of, so take off outdoor clothing before entering a building.

## Working Together

Once the eruption is over, things may be tough until the emergency services arrive to help. People will need to work together to provide everyone with:
- food and clean drinking water. Food and clean water could be scarce, so people will need to share what they have, as drinking polluted water causes sickness.
- safety: clear ash from roofs, make damaged buildings safe, and dig people out of collapsed buildings
- shelter: buildings that have been made safe may need to be opened to everyone in need
- medical care: doctors and nurses will need help from volunteers.

# QUIZ: DO YOU KNOW WHAT TO DO?

Now that you have read about volcanic eruptions, do you feel you would have a better chance of survival? Test yourself using this quiz.

**1 When is it safest to approach an active volcano?**

a First thing in the morning, while the volcano is still sleepy.

b When it has not erupted for at least 10 years.

c It is never 100 percent safe, as volcanoes occasionally erupt suddenly or more violently than anyone expects.

**2 What clues tell volcanologists that a volcano might be going to erupt in the next few days?**

a It rains a lot.

b Everyone's pet animals become cranky and irritable.

c Increased tremors deep within Earth, plus steam and gas escaping from the volcano.

**3 What volcanic product kills most people?**

a Poison gas.

b Lava.

c Ash and pyroclastic flows.

**4 If a volcano erupts without enough warning for you to evacuate, where is the best place to shelter?**

a In a forest.

b In a cave.

c In a solidly built building on high ground, but out of direct sight of the volcano.

**5 What are you most likely to need after a volcano has erupted?**

a TV, so that you have something to do while waiting for help to arrive.

b A change of clothes, plus your favorite coat.

c Food, water, and shelter.

## How did you do?

**Mostly a or b answers:** It would be a good idea to read this book again, and look at some of the web sites on the next page. At the moment, only sheer luck would save you during an eruption!

**Mostly or all c answers:** You would have a good chance of survival, and might even be able to help other people stay safe during an eruption.

### DISASTER WORDS

**volcanologists** scientists who study volcanoes

**tremors** shaking movements

**lava** liquid rock that flows from a volcano

**pyroclastic flows** hot, dense flows of volcanic ash, gas and debris collected from the ground's surface

**evacuate** leave a dangerous area

# DISASTER WATCHING ON THE WEB

*Being on disaster watch means being prepared. It also means knowing where to get information ahead of a disaster, knowing how disasters happen, receiving disaster warnings, and getting updates on what is happening after a disaster has struck.*

### Find out More about Volcanoes

Check out these web sites to find out more about volcanoes.

- **www.howstuffworks.com**
  Search for "volcano" and this site provides information on how volcanoes form, different types of volcano, different types of eruption, and even a fun volcano quiz.
- **www.weatherwizkids.com**
  Even though this a weather site, there is lots of information here about volcanoes. There are also instructions on how to make your own volcano in a soda bottle.
- **www.clearlyexplained.com**
  This site has lots of background information about volcanoes, as well as links to other sites and a button to search the Internet for "volcano news."

### Volcanoes near you

Could a volcanic eruption affect your local area, and what warning might you get? To find out, contact your local government and see whether:

- they have a volcano emergency plan
- they know of a web site you can look at for warnings of volcanic activity.

Your local library might also be able to help you find this information.

If there is significant volcanic activity in your area, this web site might be able to give you information:

- **www.pdc.org** has a live map of current disasters (including earthquakes, volcanoes, floods, and extreme storms), which you can click on to find out more. There is also an excellent resources section, with information about volcanoes and other disasters.

# INDEX